A KIND HUSBAND

By the same author

A KIND
HUSBAND

Ida Affleck Graves

Oxford   New York

OXFORD UNIVERSITY PRESS

1994

Oxford University Press, Walton Street, Oxford OX2 6DP
Oxford New York Toronto
Delhi Bombay Calcutta Madras Karachi
Kuala Lumpur Singapore Hong Kong Tokyo
Nairobi Dar es Salaam Cape Town
Melbourne Auckland Madrid
and associated companies in
Berlin Ibadan

Oxford is a trade mark of Oxford University Press

First published in Oxford Poets
as an Oxford University Press paperback 1994

British Library Cataloguing in Publication Data
Data available

Library of Congress Cataloging in Publication Data
Graves, Ida.
A kind husband / Ida Affleck Graves.
p. cm.—(Oxford poets)
I. Title II. Series.
PR6013.R33K56 1994 821'.912—dc20 94–663
ISBN 0–19–282395–7

1 3 5 7 9 10 8 6 4 2

Typeset by J&L Composition Ltd, Filey, North Yorkshire
Printed in Hong Kong

To Kristin Hughes-Stanton

Acknowledgements

Some of these poems have previously appeared in *International*, Paris, *London Mercury, Observer, Rialto, Samphire, The Spectator, The Times Literary Supplement, The Times Saturday Review*, and *Twentieth Century*; and in the following anthologies: *British Poems*, Untermeyer, USA, *PEN New Poems*, 1965.

My most sincere thanks to Peter Wallis for his help and inspiration.

Contents

POEMS

Gift

for Theodora Elizabeth Clark, Quaker Elder, 1850–1925

I love her beyond love, leave me then on the pain's spike thrust,
Tilt me then on a death void, to a dizzy and end-all downfall.
She and I, old young, without sin, blemish or piffle stumble,
Clamour, grieve to unload this, this love overspill.

Love beyond time's loving, so long idle, owns to no liar's flip
    sins,
No touch wholly trembles the fingers, tongues moist with
    silence
Wash lightly our nimble and pale smiles, I and she lit only in
    eyes
Glittering in some first particle of this loaded moment.

How to adhere, to bond a fragment, particle, a nothing,
This never-found, to puff the love breath into death, how do it,
How to twist from a mould, fungus, detritus, a new suffering
Of self herself, here the gift, snatch it, for every any sweet lover.

Daisy

To ayah, to India, to syce, mongoose
My goodbyes. The liner lit up vivid with violence,
Groaning. My sola topi wide flung into Suez,
The hooting wild ships slay me with menace.

This is grass, they say harmless, place called Boarding-house.
Worms tie in pink tangles, but who are not dry snakes.
My Ma two-times with a lover, has taffeta roses
And soft chocs. In this lush neglect I shake with terrors.

In mid-hooting and howl I fling down, my nose bruises,
Lip speared on a loose milk tooth, that ship sinking.
Then sudden, now, thumb and finger fumble a daisy
Now and suddenly know all, and all about everything.

Chrysanthemum

Goodbye to my India. I have no front teeth yet,
No chin-elastic hat, only a muslin frill bonnet.

Oily air, a slab pavement a trap to tumble on,
Here there is a place called Penge and a dread station.

On a spangled ship I guessed at death's riddles;
But what now is a gutter, why a mud mop here of petals?

Pity for it troubles me with a sharp unknown name,
Pick up love, take it to water and a new home.

Flower in toothglass, and I have grown a divinity.
Not to sob, not now laid pale alone, I sleep happy.

Carnation

Down there is a place called Penge with a forlorn station.
Thrust at me Mama's worn penny, my palm hates it.
She cries Run and run, idiot, child imbecile,
Buy him my goodbyes, a pink cake, pencil,
Carnation. Any. But not give my life's lost kisses.

My breath broken running. This was to be Play Day,
Into clay pears, matchsticks, stabs to a paper face with scissors.
Missed. So I hate him and their sobs frosty good riddance.
I adore too, stumble downhill to the whistle shriek, the roar
Of a train's pain into tunnel. No more bedtime cocoa with
    kisses.

Run and run. Station's iron pillars, roof with a petticoat frill.
A drab sells farewells. Running, ears throb with heartbeats,
Knees sting in cuts, grazes, idiot falls. Doors swing, slam.
Glimpse of fist on sill. Gladstone with labels, a coat locked in
    buttons.
The wired carnation, a pink one, I lift up, offer it.
He leans out to a red flag, says Damn, and what's that for?

Buttercup

A dead pressed buttercup. Once a park, a yellow check dress,
Toes in a sandal. Then fifty-odd turns on time's stutter,
Our time done for. Once an under-chin glow, petals' image
A fun lark of 'Yes, oh yes, Oh one does love butter,
Oh marry me, yes'; and the sun then so idle.

My handbag then had spilled its litter,
Besides the pink bus ticket, loose change in silver,
A torn letter sent of some dud homage,
A thin book fluttering fibs, ants in the grass,
Our four hands urgent to entwine this yes and yes
Pressed flower to book, into its defeat, its long shudder.

Autograph Album

Mother's album begs for a sweet something
From her chick-a-biddy on the prized pink page,
Having blue bow-wows, rhymes, bells, ever-loving
Green lies arrowed in hearts, kittens on a mauve pledge.
Lord, look what's here, what was asked for, what is got:
Matchstick gnome in irons, ankles wrists rivetted,
Squatting, claws on face, beyond all it has not,
Cell wall squared in careful ink where bone has bled.

Shut the padded album, mother gone singing downstairs
To meet a lover under a station clock,
Her chin in violets, a moist hand lusting in hers,
The doubled beast without a backward look.

Now wish her well, and with posies on the page of a headstone,
While I, her cripple, giggle and clip him in the sun.

Paraffin Stove

Suffering malaria and the spiral fall, burnt dizzy,
One's naked toe buds tethered halfway in sheet,
Orphaned by midnight I yelp noisily,
Mum at cards cannot hear my silence shout,
Bible on chair the coffin's threat,
Alphabet's gabble raves in one's throat,
Chamber-pot growls insistently.

Through the tin's slotted top
Paraffin stove prints a glowing daisy to the ceiling,
I fly up and feed on it, golden of my beginning.

The frightened aorta ticks jerkily, is blood full,
One's toe roots twist knotted to the bed-rail,
Midnight is my exploding hot farewell,
Children I call to cannot hear my bones fall,
Screwdriver on chair awaits the bell's toll,
Bible and this buzz fever threaten the kill,
Boards under the bed sawn ready.

Through the tin's slotted top
Paraffin stove flames the glowing daisy to the ceiling,
I fly up and feed on it, golden for my ending.

The White Goat

O goat, take this apple. It fell and nobody has fouled it
Or sinned and it shares this old hand's innocence.
Collar and chain tighten, the neck tassels and the rolled ears
    dance,
Juice creaks on her tongue squeezing the oval eyes to a slit
And the arcs of her horns plunge down.

Effort's rapture tilts her face for the swallow and the horns
Sweep back with the timelessness of scribbled fossils.
Up goes her lip, she bares her teeth in a laugh up-wind and
    rustles
The grass with pellets, the plume wags and her camera lens
    closes
Its pink shutters and has done.

I beg you be my Mother, for mine was nothing to speak of.
Write to me in parcels, post me snapshots, liquorice and soft
    cheeses
From home signed with udder warm hugs and kisses.
Welcome me with milk in a tall glass till I come to believe
Weeping, this love is my very own.

In the Womb

While a foetus I feed on offal and her white grief,
Her wails her swollen sobs, sick-up of a nibbled loaf,
On sips of her gin-and-it with a dim laugh;
Their exploding voices crash on my red roof.

While a mesenchyme tissue the buds of my ears,
My goggle button eyes outlining the first foes,
My twitching finger stubs, my soul's cells unfolding,
Hears the first boom and hurricane of terrors.

While an unborn I multiply in a scream,
Knees to chin in a spasm of her heart's drum;
But head first on the thread of my own pulsing
Singing sweet blood down I will come.

Dead

I am nothing, I am numbed, I am nobody,
I have none; I am yellow in the wax nudity,
The jaw bandage, the collapsed lonely nostrils,
The limp soles of my feet wrenched from gravity.

And thankfully. Please I don't need the music of spheres,
Feathers, mutter beads, nor the clip-on halo,
Nor mother's Hullo, she in a see-through bone malady
Of flame and tears, she and her Lord least of all.

Spare me this, stiff in the identity of dust.
Spare me. But before I hurtle to the hollow
Beyond this galaxy, grant me please the paws
And purrs of cats, mine, all nine of them.

Canary

Balance on it, on my knuckle, my nail-bitten small hand,
Savage it, adore, devour it. No panic nor giggles please,
His only an attack a tuft of feathers, a babe's bird claws,
Of a sweet rage or fun pecking, of a close bond.

Bird I love you more than my pearl penknife,
My flute, or my mother just moving out, better than you know who.
But beak and claws thrust in air now in this sanded cage,
His name now too sacred secret to speak of or tell you.

IN HOSPITAL

Get Well Soon

Convalescents knit coffins disasters and plots,
Grooming each other soothingly about nice weather,
A dog's tricks and once upon a time rice puddings
While they measure nylons on needles against a stomach.
It seems I have done a crime I am not aware of,
Maybe I love sweet lovers or hate my mother,
The notice reads 'Silence Please' and 'You may smoke'.

Hospital Bed

I have no weight of being, but damn well everything else,
A taut bed with the hub of my toes idling far off,
Negress and tea-trolley, roses carrying a scrum of visitors,
Hoover and Polisher humbly under and pills for afters,
Choc biscuits and a flavour of salt paperbacks in the locker,
And a nightie boiled whiter than the white of an upright stone.
But not my cat. He too has a rat-bitten spine fester
And should be in the crook of my arm to anchor
My own truth to where we can be alone together.

Ward

Nobody minds a goodbye in the iron bed
Opposite, nor the rattle of those curtain rings,
Nor the trolley, the knife, the plastic urine bag,
But I writhe, I shed my soul when two hyenas
In flowered nighties and minus their wombs
Laugh and laugh, fire the ward with laughings,
And one strikes the piano for cracked hymns.

Piano

Guess who dumbly awaits you. Give you three tries.
I do. I am a piano, my teeth on edge with lies,
Shortage of staff crepitates the ward with dead flies,
The door ajar, and you may be in for a surprise.

Blankets squared up sterilized of fluff and red fears,
Ten candlewick bedspreads obviously bored to tears,
The whiff and dark in here festers violent ideas
And fumbles for Sunday hymns. Nobody nothing appears.

I have underdamper check action, an upright,
A frame of iron, I am overstrung taut and tight,
My eighty-eight hammers await the crash of your delight.
Outside someone turns the key in smiling spite.

Visiting Hours

Here the henna teenage tart, ward bed Victory Bonny,
Curses sixpences into the telephone trolley,
Then clasps and gluts upon her own treason
Mouth to mouth with the negro's passion,
He slips chair, she jack-knifes from the pillow:
Eden's armed guard is a crafty fellow.

The Crab is lover of the next, gluts
Between skull and skin, clasps and flutters
Twice more out of her eyes while Sister
Combs hope into her hair for the visitor,
Multiplies daffodils, smiles a treason to the pillow;
Eden's sentry is a foul-tempered fellow.

This bed has the winged sandals under,
The halo a plate borrowed for dinner,
The sword stolen to halve an apple,
Flaming wrath fills a hot-water-bottle,
My visitor this time next week shares my pillow,
Eden's Angel must be a drowsy fellow.

Still-Life

In a plastic bowl oranges, choc biscuits,
Apples pleading for a green brush and a blob
Of flake white where the sun aims from a window,
Or for a knife or a bite or hand idling sideways
Even for a snatch that will knock the whole lot over.

The old woman is thinking of the Lord knows what,
Nurse with a cuppa, her boiled nightie neat with daisies,
The shop counter, mum who opened all her letters,
Maybe only waits for the sun's orange to spurt juice
And pips of rotten apples to sprout from her knuckles.

Hospital Routine

Nurse with water in glass asks sweetly
For false teeth, her fingers a pink shell held out
For this other mollusc to be grimaced out,
The plastic clappers yanked out, obediently
To her smile my smile yawned out,
My bite a bivalve in an abominable tumbler.
Scorn to her, but my own are my own,
For some two million aeons polished nightly
To nip my lover's ear, to snap his heart out.

No Wedding Ring

Nurse shrouds me in taped calico, a bag hat,
Having tested my bits and pieces, blood and heart,
Charted my religion nil, my reflexes naughty,
Shaves me for the op: table at ten-thirty.
Then rams sticking-plaster on left hand third finger,
Eyes bright with scorn, over my sin, my ring,
Set with four turquoise, with earth air fire water,
With kisses four, with four times four of laughter.

Night Duty

I died untidily, idiotically, angrily,
A wire cradle eased the itchy kiss of blankets,
But Dad's vase of daffs fell over, piddled
On the polish; I died worried about this.

As I ruckled the night-nurses swirled privacy
Round me on a rattle of curtain-rings,
Did all the necessary most silently, speedily,
Not waking others fuddled on sleeping-pills.

Done. They sit cramming exam anatomy,
Hushed, dipping into a crackle of pink biscuits.

Floating out of my cadaver my toe clumsily
Trips, bang crash go books, table, spills
Rolling biscuits, and nurses crawling on all fours
Are laughing themselves silly.

~

Horse

I, the white-winged foal, burst from the training ropes,
My hooves sparking fire in sky and over roof tops.

He who wears ram horns lassoed and leapt up on me,
I, Oxhead, led him with snorting kisses to Cathay.

The Prophet newly names me, woman now with floating mane,
Burak. We jog-ride dividing the rain, conspiring softly.

I, who clamped Old Nose Redcoat to his saddle
In battle, stood twitching in sweat till night fell.

At fourth fence I toppled my frail jockey face down,
Riderless, keeping faith with the high sky, winning the race.

Fear

Fear is a stone's sudden trip-me-up in the blank dusk,
That stone dawdling from a glacier to plot this deadly risk.

Fear the forever up and up to ultimate shudder,
Sweat of an infant's fist fast locked rigid on the ladder.

Click of the key on this cell's trap, that eye to a spyhole,
Fear in the slop bucket with all time to fill.

In the white light blaze of breath's slow strangle
All terror too dies in the final ruckle.

I fear none of these, none, never, only the smiling snow
Of the lost face of my lover at window.

I Love Myself

I love myself, my breath's ribs, my belly's view
Down to closed thighs, down to my truth-telling
Wide toes, my idle ankles, my child's vow;
Up and over the knees, the sweet bones so defiant,
So obstinate, the clever heels silent.
I love myself, I lie giving myself swelling
And admiring kisses, I adore my hair's flow,
My thighs' white mercy, the half-closed brilliance
Of eyes, I adore my cunning, and know it.

But I love one other, I worship one such other
More, yet more than self's own amaze,
More than my liar's teeth, my snow buttock,
My kisses now grazing on one another,
In that field, and beyond this barbed wire
Stands patiently the horned black bullock.

A Kind Husband

Our husband's toenails impossible to cut,
He wears a woolly insolent with sweat,
Hairs grow in the palms of his hands,
In his navel untidy puns,
The nose threatens calamity from a cliff's edge,
A limp splash and tickle its mirror-image,
Hormones claw out the majesty from his skull
The mole under his armpit corrupts all.
Forgive, for the eyes glitter with a sweet sound,
Truer than truth is a kind husband.

Our man scatters pants and tapwater on floor,
He drops the insult of old socks to make one swear,
His body in sun has no drifting ink of shadow,
He blunders crash through where there is no door,
Mirror into mirror he reflects no image,
A smear and shine only and a befuddled smudge,
His pointed teeth pleased with goading our insanity,
His breasts are void of nipples and confess no sin.
Forgive, the eyes are tender with a sweet sound.
Truer than truth is a kind husband.

Man up a Ladder

Through the window his halved legs top the ladder,
The unseen trowel taps out a mundane soft sound,
A morse to the home base criss-crossing the plaster
Where traffic's thud and plunder had made a wound.
His foot feels for the rung to go one higher,
Two sandals in air strike one as such near absence,
Suppose the sky sucked him up, a whirlwind terror
Erased him denying his very existence.
He mounts and is gone. Christ, suppose it were forever,
He has the eagle's face and the small bones for flight,
The ladder shudders, silences creak and recover,
Fear is a vacancy of air and coiled in it.
Then the ears hear the code of the smoothing trowel:
Listen, I love you, and you, and you are my all.

Man on Sewing-Machine

Leg spread he bends over a machine's murmur,
Hand under bridge between his needle's piston
And spin of woman's light wheel and tremor,
Fingers on flannel gentle between this tension.
Barge humming the echo under the black span,
Pigeon homing to scuffle under girder,
Train's homecoming to the heart's station,
These are all plain in his hand's labour.
This is brimful enough, yet not enough,
Beyond necessity one more added to all
Is hankered for, longed for, more than steel of proof,
Other than loop in thread, deeper than spool.
Here lavish on iron the gold brushes
Write it in leafy scrolls round the pearl roses.

The Kiss

You and I must amaze us, this instant, now, with a fire's kiss.
Do you know you were once beside me, behind me, above and
    below me,
Unknown in a long-ago unseen somewhere. But now No. Not
    this.

There was no other. Once we were hollows lost in a past
    nowhere
Of how, where and when. I and you separate in the stray air
Of a slow and yet slower delay. Yet now must I say No.

Why my No and No? You and I kissed, clung and devoured so
In the long-ago, our own blended nowhere somewhere,
This moment's Now is all amazed, all met.
All is Yes in this my fire's No.

Crossing Over

So I keep jump-hopping from stone to stone,
Slithering steeply, fear doubled to a buffoon,
Water's ribbed taffeta whiplashing a sandal,
Twist and danger to a left rickety angle.
But the man is safe over, has turned his back.

Stone beyond this stone is a hazarding too far,
One stride into this hissing shroud, and done for;
I lack his hand, a backward glance, a balance,
Water bludgeons me down with a silk noose,
But the man is safe over, his back turned.

The Swan

One. Her year one, dawn preens and flounces out the sun.
Swan knows how he runs to her, blown honking
Beside her in splash and beak clash, both in ripple flow.
They adore together; or surely and always must be so.

Two. Another. This new year shrugs fog and a wet odour.
Swan frets at a few far doves, paper scraps, at absence,
Maybe his feather twisted, torn claw, gunshot at his shoulder.
She holds to him, sinks low to submit, ever will await him.

Three Four. Her spring vigils alone lonely on the horizon
In coma of grief. Maybe the sun's odd blunders blind him,
Maybe, yes, a bullet sting, a net, breast to a power cable,
Swan's yellow nozzle stuns her under the white wing.

Five. Dawn sun adds five, drives her high to the skyline
To await him on the flame's edge, swan neck a loop
To delight, to define him. No, and so never. But a goose,
A grey goose, dips, curtseys to her and whirls her up.

A Widow

She takes out two forks, habit is in a daze,
One only now is needed to lay table;
The other she buries in the green baize of a drawer.

She takes down two cups, habit's one too many
At telly bedtime, rosy wreaths on bone china;
The other she slides deep into the cupboard corner.

She heaps up four pillows, three dawn aspirin,
Two habit-forming pills, one squinting prayer;
He who bored her so still fumbles in beside her.

A Husband Begs to Return

'Will you in the lost dark lie in my bed?'
No. In, onto my own pillow, fly low
Two white geese, snip and flack their wing feathers,
Then fold, settle, sleep; both they and I close and so glad.

'Will you in the wind's dark come to my bed?'
No. Duck and drake cackle in tired from the sun.
And on my pillow plot a nest and their fine weather.
My soul shuts; feathers against my cheek so good.

'Will you in woman terror slip to my bed?'
No, not likely. My bitch Muckle licks thighs, belly
And claws, rocks my pillow with dream tremors,
Makes way for the virgin goat and old horse.

'Will you in love lost relent into my bed?'
No. Would if I could. These geese, duck flutters,
Dog, horse and nanny now amaze my pillow
With a hen, with a new ten-chick sweet load.

A Lonely Widow

Should I giggle this aspidistra to window,
Or maybe push a come-hither between glass and latch,
A rolled old newspaper, a torn duster,
A crêpe flower, signals to catch some randy Mister:
Come on up, lover boy, I have a whore's gusto.
There is a smell of dead dog whom I loved so much.

Or more simply say this aspidistra lacks lustre,
Each innocent leaf sponged, needs the sun touch;
The milkman runs to the call of newspaper
With three pints; the rag snarled up in some bluster
Of wind; red poppy that once made me a widow.
Scent of the dead dog whom I loved so much.

The Rolling-Pin

You all know what it's for, for flans, for pastry
Under cracked hands, for the bandy-legged chasing
Clouting of spouses for the last cowed mastery,
Grief's music-hall laugh not of their own choosing
But of wisps of hair and the last straw.

Those lecher sailors you all know and warm to,
Rolling-pins mounting to their throats to bluster
Songs sails sweethearts, when, where, how to.
Then the homecoming wave frozen to a blister
Of blue glass with kisses galore.

But you know nothing, not yet, not the half of it,
How this sea glass is scrolled with love in harbour,
With rose garlands, with rhymes in the gold knot,
Nor seen the gift of my love's eyes in labour
Tell the untellable, and then more.

The Lithopedion

I own a Lithopedion, this a bone fossil,
A child sired by calcium upon a love-hate tussle.
A sperm's fun, a pearl grown layer on sly layer
To foetal stone, all of thirty-nine years unknown in there

Has my half-inch son inside me a soul flown out
Through the amazed top of my head, or through pink gut,
Or down on his luck, never to become a squaddy,
A gay, a lord mayor, nor never to mow the lawn on Sunday;
Or does he alone, only he, love me, so obstinately?
Yes, he is my necessity of a first and last mystery.

Poppies

This so-and-so of a man has the tidy eye on
My Poppies. Terrifies them, threatens to throw in,
Along with cabbage rot and mish-mash of old skins
And fly buzzing decay of our old sorrows
All all their scarlet flounces and swollen black suns.

This so-and-so swears they now need the chop,
These poppies, weed rubbish and trample for the tip,
Why oh why when the scarlet stuns you for love of it,
When buds know it, droop and hang meek to the blow.
Leave them alone, you, or I go too.

A Rhyme to a Girl

She sews a button on with a loose thread,
She bakes bits of grit in a sugared bun,
She blows fag-ash into the tepid teapot,
She shakes a tintack into a wellington boot,
She gulps a heartburn on a dry tongue,
She lies on crumbs on an unmade bed,
She sleeps, wakes, was, and now is not.
This She is I who has not a cloud or clue
Her sweet man has the calamity eye on you.

A Wish

She has spike teeth, hair yellow with a long sway,
Has the double delights, the cleft, the then all undone,
Christ, now could I turn into a staggering man
To bite her, and to lead myself away.

Swop Shop

Would one swop one's somewhat battered grief,
One's face, for the long blonde hair and wolf's teeth,
For the carbon monoxide of her sweet breath?

Suppose one could exchange one's worn cheese-grater
Knees and elbows for the bright ivory and glut
And sweet betrayals of her eyeballs' glitter?

Should one rip one's tongue out of its bone hutch
And swop it for the flesh of this sweet bitch
Thus proving one's own skeleton the richer?

Could one trade one's brains in as an extra,
Sign for all this, then smile into self's sweet mirror?
No point in it, I am fast asleep on the floor.

A Pebble

Pebble in a pool, in sea pool, in water glitter,
In a mirror shimmer, with echo of the white moon moist in sky.

Sand in toes, damp odours of towels, glint and glut
Of rolling seaweed, here is my infant sweet divinity.

Faraway wave voices, the blue pool's shine, eye, agate,
All blue day long the sleepers, the runners raw naked.

All is summer's spade bucket, picnic's tired clobber,
Pebble in this pool winks the tremor and lust of the lover.

This pebble mine now, dry, grey, stone only to hurl away,
Here my own wailing wet-pant infant insanity.

Sparrow

Sparrow, silly one, drab scatty infant, a claws hop-skip on the sill,
Is manic to peck glass, shrill a nonsense, provoke and slang me,
Acrobat on the narrow void of danger, regardless.

Utterly hopeless at the soul sweet rapture of birdsong,
Dud at it, has the cheek to defy, outwit the traffic kill,
The train's cry, paper-boy, this brat the bully to chirrup day long.

Sparrow, a speck's flutter, his dress nothing to speak of, no frill
On tail feathers, no scarlet, neither crest nor a ruff show-off,
But that he flies in home to my guttering it is enough.

Weeding

Weeding oh such woeful hurt, one is so bug bitten
And teased silly by the sly daft giggles of Satan.

His spite the spot tickles scarlet in agony
Of ant, horse-fly, midge, whatever he dares do to me.

The Dock's root, long as woe, deep fixed in his jaw,
Hard as one tugs at it Satan's innocence laughs the more.

Down, and down to a sunless dismay the Bellbind
Probes for earth's iron core, his satanic mind.

Nettles, Elder, Twitch threaten and crawl a serpent's ropes
And roots to grip, smother and burst my ribs.

No matter what, forget it. Weed, untangle it tomorrow.
Here the apple I promised to you so long ago.

The Marrow

They have moved house, they have gone,
Only just, for the Aga cooker is warm,
What was a welcome is now white bone,
A broomed-up whorl of dust, and Time's alarm.

Forlorn rain stutters on litter and wrenched tins,
A baby's knickers soaks in a sodden farewell,
All left out for the dustman like old sins
Confessed, exposed, and weeping on a wall.

Christ, what's this? In a bucket a marrow,
My marrow, of my growing and my giving,
Stipple sheen and stripe of green and yellow,
Drenched, thrown out of doors with all my loving.

Potato

In a paper bag in a box in the year's long flow
In the dark, total and obliterating, crouches the potato.

Silence is a white cradle meek to the unknown why or how,
Maybe the knife chop, skin to be scalped and the jaw's blow.

Why, on sudden, and by what god's command to follow
A bursting forth, night defied, does an eye's dot harden below.

The eye breaking forth down to lavish root tangles, to grow
Up up into a green density, to become my hero.

Cabbage

Look now intently at the veins, the pale bloom
Of this cut cabbage, purples of robed kings,
Green of the world's weight sap swollen,
Stem of the white heart bleached dumb.

Then silence of the soil creaking to split songs
With the lip curls of a frill, where the knife slices,
Severs, and so says goodbye to it
But not to our joined eyes.

Witch and Cat

No fuss, convulsing her claws she gave birth to seven.
Then one died. Bitterly and in fluster I lit a bonfire.
Now for some odd reason I am not to be forgiven.
She ignores me. Must everything always be my fault.

We had doted on one another. And I have no one else,
Everyone dead or dud, my heart caught and burnt out.
But scorning kisses, murmurs, her saucer, her secret name,
Back turned she suckles the six, ignoring me utterly.

The phone cut off, those snoopers back again at the windows.
Her cat cunning knows who that vivisected kitten was,
Who is to be seized by whom, why and when, by what
    neighbours,
Just who will die with her, and who precisely is to blame.

Prayer to a Cat

O Cat on the patchwork cushion complete me,
Paws in silk abandon as I would so sleep,
Inner rest of the upturned belly defend me,
The orange fire of fur melt me to hard hope.
Pin me with furled claws to the wit of patience,
Cunning slit my eyes to see all behind,
Teach me a thistledown smile to resist licence,
Pledge my strolling indifference to a true bond.
All I own is the fury of compassion,
All I now do is a goaded down-at-heel,
The forward is a backward grief of contrition,
Yesterday's tomorrow is a watery hole.
Give me your total, ignore what I have not
When crack of door opens to the rainy night.

Birth of a Kid

Goat crouches on pyramid of her own weight,
Spine's hair a crest, hollows panting
At hips; good luck telegram from Abraham
Scribbled on horns, urging her to bear down,
Balancing on udder bag, to contract grunting
If it helps, to grin and stick it out,
And if anybody laughs not to give a damn.

Grin of teeth convulses to that moist place,
Slithers out the gift in polythene wrapper
And red ribbons for hurrah, bites the release
Giving the nose breath and legs kicking ease.
Done. Now for the clean-up good and proper
And non-stop. But suddenly her tongue's grace
And charity turns and licks my fingers.

Swallow

Late, so foolishly too late, but dizzy with faith
She cements her nest with an old myth.

She unravels rags from a power-cable,
Danger in the porch and so vulnerable.

Mud and spit and energy of her throat
The fanatic's flight of a desert route.

Obstinate, high-diving among cars, lorries
And motor-bikes, the fool knows no worries.

Though the sun expires, hers the lunatic truth
Of a blind, a soon gaping yellow mouth.

Tortoise

It's a tortoise. Under the wrinkled chin stroke a forefinger.
I so desolate, so dumbly distressed, am lingering with him.

The neck wavers forth longer than his own daring,
The eye diamonds then know what they aim at and why.

Stump legs are stronger now and outgrow shell and belly
To straddle the serpent's myth and that sly garden folly.

Whatever god took up pen brushes and a frenzy of scribbles
Painted his carapace with a menace of riddles.

But under my finger's teasing this absurd sad dumb one
Hisses something, is whispering a faint song.

A Boy Digging

This garden's dead naked tangle a damn disgrace.
Whoever begs some thyme or an overblown lettuce
Risks fly-buzz, a trip-up, a thorn's dry ferocity.

A boy once digging here is lost in haze.
Bindweed thrusts down and below truth and without pity,
His hole the rubbish dump of our hearts' cold litter.

The boy digging for gold or an old coin is gone utterly.
By the rot and broken fence behold a cock-pheasant
Struts his two chuckles in a blaze of feathers.

Two Asleep

Yes, spotted mog tabby, do leap up, circle twice over
For ease, yes onto my face, for sleep, for close cover.

Sheet blanket fold us invisible as one in sleep, in soft rest,
Her belly fur obliterating both, our breathing so deeply in trust.

In trust sink yielding to her reverberation of purr,
Yellow eyes draped and close shuttered in the haw.

She the milk I the kit lulled in the single
Loud thundering unity of her fur's rumble.

Or I mother she the kit curled safe on my face, either
As one, both holy, ready for farewell on that far other.

Notes

p. 11 *Daisy*

In 1922 the liner P & O *Egypt*, carrying an immense load of gold and silver bullion, was rammed by *Seine* off Brest in the Channel and, with the loss of eighty-seven lives, sank.

p. 30 *Horse*

v. 1 Pegasus
v. 2 Bucephalus, with Alexander the Great
v. 3 Burak, with Mohammed
v. 4 Copenhagen, with Wellington at Waterloo
v. 5 The Grand National

p. 33 *A Kind Husband*

The signs and symptoms of a Wizard, a Werewolf and a Vampire.

p. 35 *Man on Sewing-Machine*

The base and body of early sewing-machines were embellished with a design of flowers, tendrils and roses.

p. 38 *The Swan*

Cobb's Bay, Lyme Regis, Dorset, 1992.
Swans mate for life.
Swan and Canadian Grey Goose are now reported as being happily together, and inseparable.

p. 43 *Lithopedion*

A dead foetus that remains in the womb becoming fossilized.

p. 56 *Swallow*

It is doubtful if the second brood survives.
A myth: where she builds her nest the home is blessed with happiness and prosperity.
She flies four thousand miles to and fro on her journey to South Africa.

OXFORD POETS

Fleur Adcock
Moniza Alvi
Kamau Brathwaite
Joseph Brodsky
Basil Bunting
Daniela Crăsnaru
W. H. Davies
Michael Donaghy
Keith Douglas
D. J. Enright
Roy Fisher
Ida Affleck Graves
Ivor Gurney
David Harsent
Gwen Harwood
Anthony Hecht
Zbigniew Herbert
Thomas Kinsella
Brad Leithauser
Derek Mahon

Jamie McKendrick
Sean O'Brien
Peter Porter
Craig Raine
Zsuzsa Rakovszky
Henry Reed
Christopher Reid
Stephen Romer
Carole Satyamurti
Peter Scupham
Jo Shapcott
Penelope Shuttle
Anne Stevenson
George Szirtes
Grete Tartler
Edward Thomas
Charles Tomlinson
Marina Tsvetaeva
Chris Wallace-Crabbe
Hugo Williams